MR PARKINSON
Poems of Love, Longing and Loss

By Gustave Dore from his illustration Tennyson's poem Idylls of the King.

Kelvin I. Jones

CUNNING CRIME BOOKS

All Rights Reserved. 2023,

OAKMAGIC PUBLICATIONS.
The right of Kelvin I. Jones to be identified as the author of this book has been asserted by him in accordance with the Copyright, Designs and Patents Act of 1988.

No reproduction, copy or transmission of this publication may be made without the   permission of the publisher, OAKMAGIC PUBLICATIONS. The illustrations accompanying this book, and herein noted as the original work of Debbie Jones and Douglas Walters remain the copyright of the artists.

Contact:
enquiries@www.oakmagicpublications.co.uk.

Table of contents

ACKNOWLEDGEMENTS VII

PREFACE IX

UNDONE 13

'YOU'RE A LONG TIME DEAD.' 15

MR PARKINSON – A MORALITY POEM 18

WOKE UP BLUES 23

I SAW THE NEWS TODAY 25

BE NOT AFRAID OF THE DARK 30

A PROSE POEM FOR MY WIFE 30

AS I STEPPED OUT ONE VERNAL MORNING 34

THE OLD BASTARDS 37

LOST ALBION 45

TWO POEMS WRITTEN AT ST JUST, 1995 53

ROCK SENTINELS 53

THE SUMMER WEDDING 53

MON FRERE, LE BATARDE, M. PARKINSON, ... 56

THE DEATH OF THE POET, WILLIAM BLAKE 63

REPO MAN 67

LUTHER'S PISS POT 77

ON THE SEA SHORE 81

HE TOLD HIS LADY... 83

A VOICE IN THE NIGHT 86

IN ANCIENT WOODS 88

I MUST GO DOWN TO THE GARDEN... 91

THE HOODED MAN 93

DREAMING OF MERMAIDS 97

AHAB IN THE PARK 102

SELDEN 111

List of Illustrations

BY GUSTAVE DORE FROM HIS ILLUSTRATION TENNYSON'S POEM IDYLLS OF THE KING. *1*

'FROM DARKNESS EMERGING,' ACRYLIC PAINTING BY DEBBIE JONES. *33*

'THE SCREAM', BY EDVARD MUNCH. *36*

PHOTO FROM WIKIPEDIA COMMONS *44*

THE SORROWS OF KING ARTHUR;' PEN AND INK DRAWING BY DOUGLAS WALTERS. *46*

PHOTO BY KELVIN. I. JONES. *63*

'REPO MAN,' PEN AND INK BY DOUGLAS WALTERS *69*

PHOTO BY KELVIN. I. JONES. *73*

MARTIN LUTHER BY HANS HOLBEIN *77*

A KENNING STONE, USED FOR DIVINATION BY CORNISH WITCHES. PHOTO, KELVIN I. JONES. *81*

'RISING GODDESS,' PAINTING BY DEBBIE JONES *83*

WOODS NEAR AYLSHAM, NORFOLK, PHOTO BY KELVIN I. JONES ... *88*

GODDESS CIRCE, STATUE FOUND IN GARDEN OF MY WIFE'S CARE HOME, IN LISKEARD. PHOTO BY KELVIN. I. JONES *91*

THE HOODED MAN - A POEM, BASED ON A PASTEL PAINTING, ENTITLED, 'THE HOODED MAN', ALSO, AN ORIGINAL POEM BY DEBBIE JONES. *93*

MERCRONE. PASTEL PAINTING BY DEBBIE JONES. *97*

LINE DRAWING BY DOUGLAS WALTERS. *102*

'SELDEN POSSESSED,' PEN AND WATERCOLOUR BY DOUGLAS WALTERS. *116*

~ vi ~

ACKNOWLEDGEMENTS

I am much indebted to my wife and soul mate, Debbie Jones, who has inspired so many of the poems in this selection.

~ viii ~

PREFACE

Let me tell you a little about myself. I'm 74 and I've had a long and varied life, My father was a strict and repressed London policeman who was part of the police campaign against Moseley's fascists in the 1930s, where he was attacked and injured by Moseley's hired thugs, the Blackshirts, and, later, processed the paperwork for those two notorious underworld villains, Ronnie and Reggie Kray, 'two expensively dressed gents in Italian suits, smoking cigars,' (his words).

My grandfather was a Victorian labourer who remembered Queen Victoria and Jack the Ripper.

I was a university student at Warwick in the 1960s, and experienced the hippy movement, its revolutionary immorality and ideas, and its fascination with drugs and sex. Here I saw many of the now legendary classic rock groups of that time performing live (The Stones, Beatles, The Who, Arthur Brown, David Bowie, The Incredible String Band, etc.).

I was taught by Germaine Greer, the famous feminist; performed in the Edinburgh Festival as the wizard, Merlin, and obtained a degree in English and American literature, entirely useless for getting a job, but handy if you were an aspiring poet, as I then was, when the 60s came sadly and disastrously to an end.

Foolishly, I then trained to become a secondary teacher of English and Drama and spent the next 26 years often regretting it. Exhausted, downcast and spiritually nullified by the age of 50, I took early retirement, left Cornwall, and wandered around Britain with my faithful wife, living here, there and everywhere.

Many years later, I came to work as a librarian at the University of East Anglia, where I also taught creative writing to adults.

In 2001, I began writing a series of ten contemporary crime novels and a biography of Conan Doyle, whose character, Sherlock Holmes, had fascinated me since childhood days. Today, I am the author of approximately 90 books, fiction and non - fiction, as a search of Amazon and Google will quickly testify.

Several critics have described me as 'a master of atmosphere, folklore and eeriness' and my work as 'not for the faint hearted.'

I have been writing consistently for over 20

~ x ~

years and, despite the onset of the insidious, crippling and challenging Parkinson's disease, do not intend giving up until the Grim Reaper finally slays me with his razor-sharp sickle

My past projects have included an annotated edition of the Victorian psychologist and sex therapist's classic work on human sexuality Krafft Ebing's *Psychopathia Sexualis* – (Dr Ebing was the first person to invent the terms Sadism and Masochism), a biography of the English lyrical poet and decadent, Ernest Dowson, (a friend of Oscar Wilde) and a book about Sherlock Holmes and smoking.

UNDONE

I have always given affection
But never asked it back,
And now I find that nothing rhymes,
And the sky's turned velvet black.

I used to chat with strangers
and listen to their fears,
But now I find I sit alone indoors
In a vale of darkened tears.

The sun's gone down into the dark,
The moon has split its cheese;
A dread corruption stalks the Earth
And there's poison in our seas.

There are white-faced men in anoraks
Peeling back the skies,
While all I touch just turns to dust,
Then, with a shiver, dies.

How could it ever go this way,
When all I sought was geniality and love,
And now I find to my dismay,
Though I was taught to kneel and pray,
That the slaughter of the innocents continues,

come what may,
And all men do sink into the clay,
And there's no heaven above.

And the world is ruled by old men in suits,
Those eminences grey
Who stand and smile as their armies salute,
Crushing the poets with their steel - capped
boots,
As the tanks roll by on Armistice Day.

'YOU'RE A LONG TIME DEAD.'

'Believe me, you're a long time dead,'
My mother used to say, that time,
Twixt Christmas and New Year,
When skies and streets
Turn charcoal grey.

When I grew old
And ceased to love,
My soul was turned by Fury,
And my heart was full of spite.
I said she hadn't got it right.
And told her she was full of shite.

When I'd turned 60,
I walked into a shop.
A mirror hung there
On the wall.
I turned, and saw a face,
Shut against
The human race,

And then I knew it all;
Remembered what she'd said.
'Son, you're a long time dead.'
But I'd set my face against the world,

MR PARKINSON IS COMING TO TEA

Her love for me which once unfurled,
Now bore flowers, black and dead.

And in her head
A church bell
Rang the orisons
Of the dead.

She'd lost her mind,
Speaking of one thing only;
That the streets were now uniformly grey,
Be it night
Or be it day.

When I heard she'd died,
I wept and said
I'd get a shirt
With bold white letters
Set against the black.
Saying
'Not yet dead.'

And Death knocks on doors,
Claiming his dues,
Demanding his rights.

When all is done
And the streets are gray
And feel like molten lead,

Now shall the dead arise
And those who could not love,
Or were not loved,
Will find no sanctuary
In heaven above,
But simply say,
'We have all this day
Been a long time dead.'

MR PARKINSON – a morality poem

Old Mr Parkinson, he fell off a wall.
Old Mr Parkinson, he had such a fall.
Old Mr Parkinson,
His poor ancient legs,
How they'd tremor and tremble.
His speech and his thoughts
He could no longer assemble.

Poor Mr Parkinson,
Those drugs that they gave him,
Made him gamble away
All his wife's hard-earned savings.

Apomorphine, they tried.
Though it gave him some relief,
Very soon thereafter
And clad only in his briefs,
He was found by police
In a brothel
In Pon Ty Pryff,
With a girl, who was giving him
Hand relief.

Poor Mr. Parkinson,
He didn't last long after that.

He was stranded,
Sometimes stressed,
Sometimes even rabid,
In a dismal flat.
Living there
Year after year, unaided.

They found him at last, alone,
In a stinking bedsit.
His clothes smelled of urine.
And poor old Mr Parkinson -
This made matters even worse, you see-
He was covered entirely
From top to toe, in shit.

Once the doc had examined
The state of the corpse
Someone rang for an ambulance,
Then and there, of course;

And here's another
Tragical, comical,
Comical tragical, matter of fact.
It took altogether
Four hours and three ambulance men
To get him out of that flat.
They had to take out a window
There and then
Since he'd grown so prodigiously fat.

MR PARKINSON IS COMING TO TEA

He'd lived on a diet
Of chips and cheese,
You see,
Topped with lashings
Of marrowfat peas,
While the bottle of pills
They'd prescribed, levodopa,
In a moment of either despair or anger,
He'd flushed down the loo
Or hurled over the sofa.

Now by the time the consultant
Arrived in his Porsche,
And he'd left his rich chums at the local
golf course,
Mr. P had died
And no one showed a flicker of remorse.

'That's the thing with the oldies,'
Said a man with a grimace.
'They cost the NHS a lot;
And take up far too much space.'

Oh, poor Mrs Parkinson,
For her fate was no better.
They sold off her home
to pay back the council
All the money Mr P. then owed
On the never never.

And that's not all.
Now his wife sits alone
In an old people's home.
Each day she speaks to no one,
And has no one to speak to
Or call
And her face has turned to stone.

Old Mr Parkinson,
He sat on a wall.
Old Mr Parkinson,
He had such a fall.

So much of his life
Fell apart, or was denied.
Tormented and taunted
by his Lewy Dementia,
He'd sit in his flat
Where most days he'd curse and cry
At his life of sad misadventures;

For despite the advice
Of those clever neuro surgeons
And the talented, medical, professional men
Who'd advised Mr P.
To take levodopa
Dead on the hours of 6 and then ten,

No matter what pill or what medicine they

MR PARKINSON IS COMING TO TEA

prescribed,
It cannot be denied,

They just couldn't put
Mr Parkinson
Back together again.

WOKE UP BLUES

Woke up this morning,
Feeling kinda rushed.
A thousand souls accumulatin'
Cemetery dust.

Woke up late this morning,
Wished I hadn't done.
The Grim Reaper's Fight to Kill
Has only just begun.

Woke up late this evening,
Feeling real low,
Watched the crematorium chimney's
Phosphorescent glow.

Walked into the desert
Where Christ used to go.
Where Jesus once grew flowers,
Now only black weeds grow.

Woke up this morning,
Sold the Cadillac,
Then walked to my apartment
And painted it black.

MR PARKINSON IS COMING TO TEA

And now there's nowhere to go;
I ain't turning back,
For my soul feels like a dead man
On a railway track.

And in the heart of every city
And the heart of each man
Is a sharp steel dagger
And a deadly plan,

When Judgement Day will bury us
With mortar fire and shell,
To cut the ground from under us
And take us all to Hell,

For the Lord thy God
Is a vengeful God,
And His Will shall be done,
Until His flame and brimstone
Hath consumed
Each and everyone.

KELVIN I. JONES

I SAW THE NEWS TODAY

'Nonmotor symptoms may require additional treatment in many people. Parkinson's disease itself doesn't cause death. However, symptoms related to Parkinson's can be fatal. For example, injuries that occur because of a fall or problems associated with dementia can be fatal.'- from an NHS advice leaflet.

I saw the news today,
Oh man.

10,000 tickets sold for Parkinson's.
And though the Albert Hall was full,
I couldn't get there.
I knew that if I tried,
I'd simply fall.

I sat at home and cried.
To cap it all
A bomb went off
In Marylebone
At just past nine
On Tuesday night

MR PARKINSON IS COMING TO TEA

And killed them all.
I saw the news today,
Oh man.

A wealthy businessman
Had Parkinson's.
And though the news was rather dire,
He didn't once perspire.

He bought a petrol can and then,
To his adoring wife just said,
'I'm driving down to Beachy Head.
When you wake up, I'll be dead.'
She phoned an ambulance.

But things turned out like he said.
And down by Beachy Head that night,
The sky turned red.

I saw the news today,
Oh man.

A plane to Canada
Fell out the sky.
Two hundred people
Burned to death.

I had a ticket for that flight.
I searched and searched for it

All night.
If I'd been on that plane,
I'd have done it right.

I saw the news today,
Oh man.

A man from Bristol
Took a carving knife.
He got a taxi to
To the Brunel bridge,
And slashed his throat, then jumped over it.
The head came off
And hit a boat.

His grief- racked mother
Found a note.
He'd had Parkinson's for years
But not once explained to her his fears.

'Must have been terrible,
And now he's dead.
Why does God always piss on us?'
She said.

I saw the news today,
Oh man.

Some wealthy author

MR PARKINSON IS COMING TO TEA

Got a Booker prize.
He blew his brains out
In his sports car.

He'd travelled long
And lived too far.
For ten long years
He'd told his Parkinson's
To stuff itself.
Now all his books are off the shelf,
And there's no one in heaven
Who likes his stuff,
No one but himself.
No one wants to read him
Anymore.
Said his wife,
'He was a self pitying bore,
Hanging about at parties,
Consorting with whores.'

Look,
I'm going to the bathroom
With a razor and stack of pills.
I won't be very long.
And when you next clap eyes on me,
After the funeral
I'll be
Like a withered leaf
On a long dead tree,

long gone, but finally,
Of Parkinson's
I will at last be free.

BE NOT AFRAID OF THE DARK
A prose poem for my wife.

And I said to myself be not afraid of the dark
for the dark will come to you in many guises
like a batwing flapping in a hall of
disconnected memories he will arrive in a
winter storm his black cloak just visible
through a stand of ancient trees he will come
to you unannounced like a pale spectre at the
celebratory feast his spectral fingers beckoning
from the shadows but I say again be not afraid
of the dark for jurisdiction hath he none in the
land of the living he will come and perturb you
in the din of homeward bound traffic at the
point of reckoning when your hopes fail when
you know you'll not make it home at the hour
of his summoning his thin hand pulling you
into the shadows and draining your courage
but I say again be not afraid of the dark he
shall lie in wait for you on the road less well
travelled his oaken staff flailing the cold black
air summoning the spirits of the long dead and
departed a ragged tattered creature his hollow
eyes closing in on you in the gathering gloom
but he dare not break into the sunlight that
surrounds you for he is not of this world and

you shall stand at the crossroads forbidding
him the gibbet and the hanged man's bony grip
all the while gathering the sunlight into you
and I said to myself be not afraid of the dark of
the long drowned man with eyes full of sand of
the woman cut down in her prime of the child
unborn or misbegotten of the brother who
could face no more pain who smothered his
sorrow with a semblance of suicide I say be not
afraid of the dark for the dark shall come to
you when you least suppose him like a flail in
a field of cropped corn scattering your seed
grinding your precious memories into dust but
he has only the strength of your fear of him
and the weight of your past sorrows and the
dark hath no dominion so I say once more be
not afraid of this sad spectre this grim
apparition this lost spectre of melancholy mist
this harbinger of sorrow be not afraid of the
dark for the dark has no substance and no
skin of the living no gut no red umbilical cord
for his domain is down in the stone cold earth
where the dead man lives on in purgatory
regretting those he had not loved or those he
had spurned and cast asunder for that man
chose not to live in the guts of the living for he
was afraid of the dark and the dark set sail in
his sorrow and fear and so I say again be not
afraid of the dark for he dare not come to you

MR PARKINSON IS COMING TO TEA

in the light nor can he smile or weep or revel in
your peal of laughter nor can he stand to
watch the burning sphere of the sun as it rises
so I say again be not afraid of the dark begone
dread dead creature of fear for you have no
right to be here and we cast out your shadow
for we are many and we live in hope not
despair for we live and we love in the daylight
and we dwell in the glorious light of the radiant
summer sun.

'From darkness Emerging,' acrylic painting by Debbie Jones.

AS I STEPPED OUT ONE VERNAL MORNING

As I stepped out one vernal morning,
Through meadows burned by a piercing sun,
The hills lay wrapped in a golden haze,
The sky, a shining bowl of blue.

A brown hare ran
Athwart me, its blue eyes flashing,
Its long lank ears like gyroscopes,
Twisting and twitching
As it passed.

Above me, birds of every hue
Carolled their voices at my advance,
Announcing my clumsy progress
To their kingdom of duck and dab.
I glimpsed her in soft morning shadows,
Half visible by an ancient yew,
Her golden tresses decked with roses,
Her limbs kissed by morning dew.

She smiled, then waved,
But in an instant
Was lost amid the trees,
Her lissom legs smelling of blossom,
Her step as light as a soft Spring breeze.

Sometimes, when stirring from slumber
That vision returns to me,
Here in her sylvan presence,
Here, where the *genius loci*
Whispers her name among the trees.

For my world is grim and filled with sorrow,
And the hare moves no more across the
meadow.
And I wake from dreams of my vernal goddess,
Half sick of woodland faery shadow.

And here in the valley below me
Where no birds sing,
They are binding the trees
With barbed wire and string.

MR PARKINSON IS COMING TO TEA

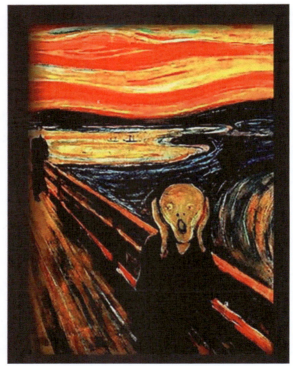

'The Scream', by Edvard Munch.

KELVIN I. JONES

THE OLD BASTARDS

*A poem for the lost generation. With apologies to
Kingsley Amis,' The Old Bastards.'*

1.

Others there did stand,
70 years too late,
With no more time to celebrate.

Once we were couples,
Friends at uni.
When love conquered all,
And summer days were groovy.

But now we're old,
Love's turned to hate,
And we sit at home and cogitate.
Washed up, in the washing up,
Bodies turned to fat,
By long passages of time,
We sit, writing poetry
That doesn't rhyme.

"A burden on the taxpayer,"

MR PARKINSON IS COMING TO TEA

They shout
As we drift about,
"Always getting in the way."

Sometimes
They glimpse our cars in lay - bys,
Nodding off at night;
We took the wrong route, here on the left,
Not here on the right,
Searching for that which we once had,
And now is not in sight.

In the Memory Cafe, up from Spar,
They don't remember who they are.

They don't recall their kith and kin.
They don't recall a bloody thing.

"You're a burden on the welfare state;
God's waiting room is running late.

"You've had it all
And you've no more time.

"Old bastards, you are,
Not worth a dime."

2.

After Wendy died,
And Uncle George at her funeral,
Mortified,
Sat down and cried,
Things were never quite the same.

Sister Alice, who had dementia,
Sat talking of her 'Golden Palace,'
And her long- lost sons,
And of her cousin Rosie
Who died in a knife attack,
Not far from here,
Found lying in a gutter,
Her face beaten black,
Shortly after the pubs had closed.

Rose told her
She'd met her two young sons,
Those lovely boys
Who died so young,

And Alice said,
Her world was now bereft
Of music, laughter and song.

3.
Wendy would sit in her garden,
Carving
Small bone objects, like sailors once carved,
But then were lost on storm - wracked days,
Drowned
Beneath the foam-tipped waves.

Here in her garden,
Here on Wendy's reverential ground,
She prayed she'd meet
The souls of the departed
Who gathered here at Pentecost.

Not far from where Wendy sat,
Were two tall angels
With skins as white as alabaster.
They reached out to her and cried.

Never before had she
Heard women cry like that;
They wept and moaned and gnashed their
teeth.

Wendy feared to disturb them,
Lest they die in their sleep,
And then could not return
To paradise;

That place of rare beauty
Where they only let in
Good Christian sinners
Who'd done their duty,

But no mercy for Wendy,
Not on days
When Wendy had been bad,
Or on days she felt
She was turning
Slowly mad.

4

In those times of confusion and despair,
When Wendy felt she was no longer there,
She met her husband in the conservatory,
Filling in forms,
His face forlorn.

He told her
He couldn't remember;
He couldn't quite recall,
Who he was at all.

When poor Alice,
Later on that night,
Stood in her garden,
Her clothes rent and ragged,

MR PARKINSON IS COMING TO TEA

Soaked through with sweat,
She heard stars weeping in
The firmament;

That same night,
When her husband's lips turned blue,
He had sat reading Dickens
In the garden shed 'til two,
When the neighbourhood was dead,
And nothing moved.

After this, Arthur didn't seem
Like Arthur,
But lay next to her in bed,
Listening to the voices in his head.

Then Wendy knew, like all of us,
That it was true;
Her life had suddenly
Been split in two,

And she lay now in the dark half,
Where no one ventures through.

"I wish I lived near my Golden Palace,"
Said Wendy,
"I wish I were like Alice,
In that book where things grew
More magical,

Hour by hour.
Come to the garden,
Help me to lament,
For my husband is dead,
And the sun is in the night sky
And has turned
A burning red.

"And once, where there was a Paradise,
Angels oft do weep,
And their tears fall like pebbles
In the resounding deep.

"For us, there's no resurrection
Nor Christian heaven sent,
For the sun no longer shines
In the firmament."

MR PARKINSON IS COMING TO TEA

Photo from Wikipedia Commons

LOST ALBION

This poem was inspired by a vivid dream I had in the summer of 2021, after I had been studying a painting by Debbie Jones, *painted by her in 2011.*

All that night long, it seemed to me,
The noise of battle clanged and dinned,
Til I awoke and saw the fallen Arthur,
His side riven,
His guts spilled on a rock.

And beside him
Stood Bedivere, the Judas knight
who could not throw Excalibur into
Dozmary Pool.

As daylight spread its filigree of pallid silk
Across the sleeping landscape,
I took the path up to the moor.

It was then that I met him.
Not a knight of Arthur,
But a miner,
Weary and disconsolate,
From his nightly chore.

This ancient man
Commanded me to stop,
Raising thus his hand.
Then I saw that close behind him,
Others too did tread,

The sorrows of King Arthur;' pen and ink Drawing by Douglas Walters.

Their clothes rags and tatters.
Their countenances grim,
And bathed in sweat.

"Sit down and listen", one did say.
"There is much to hear before the breaking of
the day.

"Once this was a green and pleasant land.
Before the building of those dark Satanic Mills,
that still do stand.
But long before we came,
Lucifer had other plans.

"Long and painful was our chore as we worked
in the damp and the dark,
Bent double, stripping and blasting the living
land.

"We were the Hard Rock Men,
The diggers and the blasters of granite.

"Our Infants coughed up soot.
There were scars, and weals
Where rocks had hit us on the back.

"We worked in mud and dust, from dusk to
dawn,
In stinking mire,

MR PARKINSON IS COMING TO TEA

Till our bodies
Were but scars and blackened husks,

"So that our Lords and Masters might
Quaff at the tables of the rich.
And the pampered slave masters of Bristol
Could grow ever more flatulent and grand,

"As we grim men carved granite.
From the bowels of the earth below;
Our days spent in darkness,
Lit only by the Davy lamps' fitful glow."

He paused,
Then,
As birds began
Heralding the coming dawn,
He sighed, then spoke again:

"This nation was not made great
By wigged Tories
And their avaricious schemes,

"But by miners who beat and hammered
These tin - rich seams
Until their lips were blue
And their tongues laced with arsenic.

"Then, when the work ran out,

We Cousin Jacks left these shores.
Our days were through.

"Those who stayed on starved, or
Joined up to fight the cause of war.
Since they had little else to do.

"We travelled far and wide across the globe,
Digging ore.
We dug the trenches,
Made love to foreign wenches.

"We heard the German cannons wail,
Then crash above in the soot- drenched,
Blackened air.
And each morning gathered to hear
The orison for the dead
As razored shrapnel
Rained down on our heads.

"We saw them die like cattle
In places such as Passchendale and Mons.
Those few who remained came back
With tales which could not be told
And sleep turned to nightmare.

"When those bloody scenes
Returned in dreams,
Those who survived had little to say.

MR PARKINSON IS COMING TO TEA

Our tales were buried with the dead.

"So each night we walk here
"Until break of day
And cross these muddy fields,
Seeking to understand
What became of Kernow,

"That once tree-lined land
Of holy wells and fairy lore
Where Arthur sat by Dozmary Pool
Mortally wounded by his son,
Betrayed even by his closest right -hand man."

Here I glanced up and saw
A light piercing the already
Leadened sky,

And saw then a shape
Like an angel
But bearing wings
Of blackened skin.

And I knew then,
The curse which had doomed Arthur,
Also had doomed my weary traveller,
Trapped here in purgatory,

And that his wounds would bleed again,

Gush forth like the poison, which forever
Leaks and leaches
From this fractured earth of Cornwall,
This scarred and pitted land;

For the land demands its sacrifice,
And those who strip it bare,
Are, in time, crushed by its remorseless hand.

He nodded his farewell
And all fell silent behind him.

Then at once, we heard
A sound far off,
Like
The beating of the wings
Of a thousand carrion crows,

Swooping to the earth below them,
Ravaging and plundering the soil.
In a blackened and gathering shroud they flew
And onwards, beyond,
Across fields of the living
He would never know.

Then, as the carrion crew flew over us,
I saw in an instant,
The Hard Rock revenants had departed,

MR PARKINSON IS COMING TO TEA

And I was left, standing
In a muddy field
Alone,

Thinking of those
Who bore the shards of shattered
Lives and memories
Upon their arms and ribboned backs;

Those Hard Rock Men
Who worked the granite rock,
With faces crystalline and deathly white,

Here, where I stood above,
While they toiled on in darkness,
Whence they'd come,
To haunt me
From deep below.

KELVIN I. JONES

TWO POEMS WRITTEN AT ST JUST, 1995

ROCK SENTINELS

Beaten by winds,
Yet still entire,
Old bones, green - hued,
Hung out to dry
On earth's crust.

Pummelled, cracked
Into gnawn ribs,
They face west,
Their hearts glittering,
Enduring frost and tempest,
Their flesh grist.

THE SUMMER WEDDING

From the doors of the hotel they process,
Young, old and beautiful,
Correctly but casually dressed.

It is the morning after the wedding.
Faces fixed in repos;
Hands clutching bags and cameras.

MR PARKINSON IS COMING TO TEA

The handfasting has come to a close.

It is the morning after the wedding.
What is done now may not be undone,

And all the while behind them,
Waves flecked with white tongues,
Rocks like sentinels,
Burnished by the late July sun.

Bridal bouquets lie on tables,
Wilting in air - conditioned heat.
Old men pose awkwardly by polished cars,
Their children manicured and neat.

It is the morning after the wedding.
Guest start to drift away.
The sun carves an arc across the ocean,
And night drives its scythe into day.

And all the while behind them
Is heard the symphony of sea and sand,
And the ritual of departure
Is the placing of hand in hand.

Presents wrapped in polythene,
Placed carefully in a car,
A ring encircling a finger;
The proclaiming of who we are.

The promise of immortality,
The partner in our bed.
Baptism marriage and funeral,
By these certainties are we led.

Cars wind back up the coast road,
Wind heralds sudden rain.
Holding hands in the wedding car;
The kiss that shares another's breath.
Birth, baptism, marriage, death,

And the sea rises and plunges,
And we drown and die in its spume,
And the shore is never the same shore twice,
And their lives shall never be the same once
more,
Nor shall they ever be again,

As they stand here, loving bride and groom,
Hands gripped like a vice,
On that sun-blessed
Land's End afternoon.

MON FRERE, LE BATARDE, M. PARKINSON, AND WHAT WE DID TOGETHER

Canto One: Bristol.

Lost on The Downs
With driver Jack.

On Isambard's bridge,
The ravine beneath
Invites me to jump,
Threatens to engulf.

No going back.

Finally,
In the wilderness
Of Bristol's storm - etched streets,
The Brain Centre declares its function.

'Might I have a new one?'
I quip.
But Jack ignores
My unmitigated bleat.

A silent waiting room.
A silent specialist.
He speaks in halting English
And fixes me with eye and pen,
I, the patient,
He the neuro - Olympian.

'Not just the Parkinson's.
There's something else besides,
And this troubles me...'

He positions his pen
As if to sever an artery.
I want to reply, jokingly;

'Oh yes? Please DO tell.'

Now an insidious voice at my back,
A shifting and clattering
Of old bones.

Mon frere. Le batarde.
He knows me well.

Outside, we cross the road
Storm - torn by rivulets of rain.

And then the slow return,
My driver silent,

MR PARKINSON IS COMING TO TEA

Driving down the dark,
As if to Hades bent.
Sometimes I see his face,
My invisible doppelgänger.
From the back seat,
It's thin, cadaverous;
And for a second,
I glimpse his sneer.

He's still with me.
Still here.

Canto 2

I knew I had seen that face before.
I had seen it in my troubled waking dreams:

The aquiline nose, the forehead domed,
The hands white and fine,
The mouth fixed and cruel,
The sharpened fingernails
Polished and thin.

'Today I looked at your tests,' said he, the
neuro,
In a whispered voice of menacing timbre,

A voice of one who had lived for centuries,
From the time of Attila and Alexander.
I did not desire to hear the rest.
He told me the twitching of my thumb
Was but one insignia of my fate,
And that our fifteen years spent together
Would form a contract of enduring hate.

Outside my apartment, dusk slowly thickened,
Small birds fell and died in trees,
But his keen eyes closed upon my face,
As he catalogued the symptoms
Of this crippling disease;
The dystonic hand, the violent cramps,
The rigidity of limb and face,
And I was ill at ease;
Whilst behind him
I glimpsed, in my vision,
Whales and dolphins
Dying in agony in the raging waves
Of blood- wrecked and consuming seas.

He was smiling as he spoke,
Savouring his every word,
A routine performance he'd given before;
He'd stood in mute and grim attendance,
As some, in dire depression,
Had hung themselves, or crashed their cars
In fast lanes on motorways,

MR PARKINSON IS COMING TO TEA

Or drank themselves to death in bars,
Whilst others took the drugs prescribed,
Knowing only surgery would succeed
In reducing the torture of their plight.
Some became sexually addicted, others
gambled;
Some fell into depression;
One became wildly deranged,
Shot at his wife and blew her brains out,
Having arranged his suicide.

I sat and listened quietly
As he completed this litany
Of darkness and death,
Aware that the room was growing colder,
Knowing he would never leave me,
Until I surrendered my very last breath;

I watched with mounting repulsion
This grey apparition,
This locust who would dog and stalk me,
Winnowing my strength year on year.

I found myself
Staring at his fleshless ears
And the grey pallor of that grinning face;

And then, far off in distant hills
I heard the howling of ravenous wolves.

Those children of the night,
What music they made
In that cold, still but deadly moonshine
Compounded of my doubts and fears.

They sang and sang,

Whilst, I, with dread trepidation
Heard ancient trees in the deep forest fall
And the rocks trembled,
And cemeteries yielded the living dead;

Here in my room, the spectre's hand
Crept across my freezing shoulder,
And there, on the misty horizon,
I spied the rusted gates of Hell.

Now fifteen years later,
The wolves grow in number;

Locked in my body, I sit in my room
And watch and wait.

And each year
The wolves grow louder

And he grows stronger.
Parkinson; that benefactor of the human race,
The arbiter of my fate,

MR PARKINSON IS COMING TO TEA

That tattered, scabrous revenant
Who in time I would come to loathe and hate.

Photo by Kelvin. I. Jones

THE DEATH OF THE POET, WILLIAM BLAKE

Blake went into the garden
To sit there with his wife
And Blake saw God in the garden,
Who was talking to Adam's wife.

And Blake made love to Adam's wife,
There in the garden beneath a burning sun,
And then he saw that he had defiled Eve
And would be cursed each time

MR PARKINSON IS COMING TO TEA

That he made love.
Then God told Blake he must renounce the
Devil
And follow the path of love, not hate,
But the sunlight had changed to murk and
mist,
And he saw his own dark shadow
Among the shadows,
Gathering there at the garden gate.

And when Blake turned his face to the
heavens,
He heard the trilling skylark there.
But when Blake went again to the garden,
He was damned by grief and despair.

And Blake heard the miners
hammering rock,
Deep in the bowels of the bleeding earth,
And he knew then the time of Ragnarock
Was as certain as death and birth.

Blake told his wife before he died
He was weary of life and toil,
That the sun would sink beneath the night
And the oceans would boil
With blood and oil.

For God now lay dead in the garden,

Branded with the Devil's mark.
Blake had brought death to the garden
And the sky was twisted and dark.

Blake's wife saw Satan in the garden,
And found she could no longer pray
And saw the flowers were stripped and bare,
And the Devil went nightly there
To stand with the dead on Judgement Day.

Then Blake was buried in the garden
And black clouds did fill the sky,
And Blake's wife would not sit in the garden
For fear that she might die.

She saw then the Devil in the garden
And saw the flowers were stripped and bare,
And the Devil he danced nightly there
Naked as the dead on Judgement day.

And others then came to the garden,
And they put up a stone to mark his grave.
Blake sat at the gates of purgatory,
Alone and naked for all to see,
Cast out by God for eternity.

For Blake had seen God in the garden,
And his face was white and hardened,
Bleached as weathered bone,

MR PARKINSON IS COMING TO TEA

Rising clear and white as the harvest Moon.
And God was singing the Devil's tune,
And his finger was pointing to Blake alone.

REPO MAN

I'm sorry that I missed you.
I'm sorry you were late,
I'll catch you when you're next in view,
Or just about to emigrate,
Yes, I'm the promised man,
I'm the Last Post man.

I left my card in your letterbox,
So please don't scream or shout,
Or close your doors, or change the locks;
I'll always be about.
I'm the repo man
Yes, your repo man.

I'm the guy you spotted on the road
Who almost isn't there,
The old guy in the musty clothes
Who's gasping out for air.
I'm the no hope man,
The fast disappearing man.

I'm the one you least expect,
When your window blinds are down,
My eyes are stained, and sorrow flecked,
I'm the man in sombre brown.

MR PARKINSON IS COMING TO TEA

I'm the calling card man,
The joker in the pack man.

My invitation to the dance
Is almost every place.
My calling cards are edged with black,
And on the obverse there's a space,
So you can call me back.
I'm the endgame man,
The post – it - note man.

I'll book you in for Tuesday next;
Your name is in my book.
You'll know me by my twisted look,
The one you least expect.
I'm the repo man,
The man by any other name man.

I'm the person who you never met,
The one who came too late,
The author of catastrophes,
The harbinger of fate.
For I'm the nowhere man,
The hard to bear man.

I'm the man who walks without a sound,
The man in the Pacamac,
The Father Christmas come to town
With babes tied in his sack.

I'm the exit man,
The many sorrows man.

I'm the guy who comes at eight
You'd arranged to see at ten,
The man you've dodged and learned to hate,
And you won't be coming back again,

'Repo Man,' pen and ink by Douglas Walters

MR PARKINSON IS COMING TO TEA

For I'm the late entry man
The post haste man.

I'm the man who steps right in
Where angels fear to tread.
The demon in the rubbish bin
Who fills your dreams with dread.
I'm the odd job man,
The dreaded, dead
Knock on the doorman.

Some meet me when they're very young,
And others when they're old.
My eyes are blue and deadly cold,
My lips are white and tightly spun,
With broken hearts, I'm told.
I'm the dead - end man,
The soul repossession, man.

My flesh peels off like parchment,
My heart is sooty black.
They'll say it's sad you ever went
But you won't be coming here again,
And won't be coming back.
For I'm the end of the line man,
The end of time man.

When all's well, that ends well,
You'll know I'll wait for you,

When your throat or tongue begins to swell
Or your lips start turning blue,
For I'm the not forgotten man,
The unforgettable blue man.

It's me who keeps the numbers down.
You'll know when I'm around.
I'm the one who's coming here for tea,
You'll know it's me;
You'll hear my shuffling sound,
My step like slow eternity,
My voice like stifled sound.

I'm the clown with the death mask,
And the leprous left hand.
I'm the long - forgotten man
They never thought to ask.
Yes, I'm the groundhog man.
I hover on the motorways,
Seeking out the dead by chance,
Hoping you'll glimpse my skull face there
And my bone - rattling dance.
I'm the dread collector,
The chalk - white spectre man.

I'll seek you here, I'll seek you there,
I'll seek you everywhere.
I'll seek you when you're cold and bare,
And your heart fills with despair.

MR PARKINSON IS COMING TO TEA

I'm the finishing line man,
The Exocet missile man.

You'll wish you hadn't seen me
When I show up in the crowd,
For you'll never then be free of me,
And then I'll shout out loud:
'I'm the grim reaper; the mortician man;
The long dead, Rip Van Winkle sleeper man,
And I've come to collect you,
And I'll not forget you.
And my scythe is ready in my hand'.

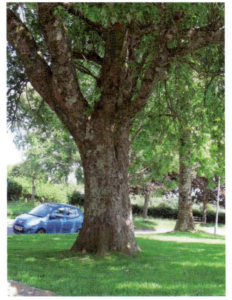

Photo by Kelvin. I. Jones

IF THERE IS A GOD

If there is a God,
Then perhaps
He's some malign,
Humourless trickster,
It occurs to me.

They call it dementia.
I call it a catch - all phrase,
A mere hand me down,

MR PARKINSON IS COMING TO TEA

A make - do,
An excuse, sometimes;
To humiliate me,
To pull the plug on me
In front of friends.

A cruel twist from her
Emerging dark side,
Like a diver, coming up
Through murky waters
With the bends.

To her fading mind,
I am the lodger,
The scarcely recognisable friend,
The man in her attic,
Lost in time;

He who, years past,
Replaced her mythic husband,
The one who forgives her transgressions,
The one who wearily makes her amends.

Or maybe, in her more lucid dreams,
I am like some shambling,
Misbegotten, shuffling apology
For who I once was,
A rickety tin man,
Creeping his loathsome path

Back to Bethlehem.
Was it some sickening joke,
When Christ hung upon the cross,
Then so slowly gagged and choked?

Fifty years married,
And still inexplicably celibate,
I know her not,

This woman who recalls naught
But shadows of her past,
Clutching at straws,
As the fractured gleams of
Thought and time
Rise, then sink to nothingness,
Down into the dark.
Was it all a joke,
This so - called Divinity of Man?
Perhaps those who saw him hanging there,
And heard him choke,
Who cried out to him,
"Ecce homo! Behold the man,"
Glimpsed in that moment
The truth we never can;

In her disordered world
Of fading light,
There is some faint memory
Of who I once was,

MR PARKINSON IS COMING TO TEA

Or who I might have been,
And how I now am,
A ghost or echo lost.
A drifting revenant.

Day is over;
Once more we're
In the dark,
Wishing we might be
In the sun.

I pause for sleep,
Ready to face with her
Another day;
The joke is done.

But as i turn the lamp off,
I see Him hanging there,
His tortured face smeared with tears,
Ready to face eternity
Upon the Cross.

LUTHER'S PISS POT

Martin Luther by Hans Holbein

It appears to me
A curious dilemma,
Is it not,
As I sit here in the privy,
On the pot,

That once I had thought God not to be God,
But an aspect of my mind's derangement,
But now I am certain it is not.

Here on the pot,

MR PARKINSON IS COMING TO TEA

Twisting and turning,
But producing not a jot,
I see it is the Devil that has damned me,
Brought me down,
To this state of perpetual constipation;

My body's in a state of disarray,
So afflicted, I cannot even pray,
Despite my constant semiotic ratiocination.

Now, it seems, I cannot tell
If there ever was,
Or whether
There is or is not
A God who forgives my sins,
My constant veniality,

Or may have cursed me thus
In the fundamental section
Of my musings,
Thus reducing, *ad absurdum,*
The divinity of creation
To the contents of a chamber pot.

I know not how I know it,
Whether it be
By divine inspiration,
Or some arcane form of polyglot,

But of this I'm very certain:
That about an hour from now,
I shall still be on this chamber pot,
And Lucifer will still be here;
Whether I wish him to be here or not.

I'm so freezing cold, I quiver,
Yet there is one stygian spot,
One part of my anatomy
That feels as hot as hell
And pained, branded and afflicted
By His demons' prod.

You ask what it is?
I would have thought that obvious,
Like that white stain on your surplice.

I've been talking to My Maker
Of matters theological,
Of the enigmatic paradigm of Time,
Of why the Devil plagues me thus,
And why some poems simply will not rhyme.

I know I'm late for vespers,
Brainless Brother Lucas.
Stretch your hand above this privy door,
Grasp this piss pot, now empty it,
While I wipe the smile
From the face of His Satanic Majesty,

MR PARKINSON IS COMING TO TEA

For I care not a jot
For your face either,
Brother Lucas,
You unobservant clot.

ON THE SEA SHORE

A kenning stone, used for divination by Cornish witches. Photo, Kelvin I. Jones.

Once, when standing by the seashore,
You reached into the foam
And plucked forth a shining stone.

A quartz pebble;
Soft and smooth it was,
Shaped by centuries of crashing waves.

In its glinting iridescence
You glimpsed other worlds

MR PARKINSON IS COMING TO TEA

More remarkable than this,
Locked in mystery, full fathom deep.
Would that I possessed your scrying eye
Or might catch those visions you espied.

HE TOLD HIS LADY

'Rising Goddess,' painting by Debbie Jones

He told his lady thus:
'In thy sweet mouth
There is such deliverance,
My lady.

In thy sweet smile
There exists a world beyond
To which, for certain,
Only you and I do hold the keys
A world of amorousness
In which long embraces

MR PARKINSON IS COMING TO TEA

And kisses ardent and passionate
Do we trust,

Until such time
As the sun divine
Plummets to earth and burns,
And oceans turn to rust.

Give me, then,
Those rose - drenched lips,
That I may quench my own lips,
Thus and thus,
Until virtue is lost forever
To both of us.

Then shall we two say,
When virtuous folk
Speak ill of us,
Or prick our teats
For proof the Devil dined with us,
And left replete,

"Thou wast not there.
Thou never tasted lips so fair,
Thou never lingered
On her locks of golden, sun-kissed hair".

And when, at last,
At ending of day,

He lost her and came home
By way of wood enchaunted,
And past a mere, where the living
Dare not linger long at dusk,

How they do dread
His cold, dank touch, saying to him:

"She was of the faery folk
Whose bones lie buried there
Beneath the hill,
Where she and her kind
At dead of night, do roam there still.

"They say her clothes,
Now rags and tatters,
Do smell of long dampened hay
And of rancorous, garnished offal.
That holds a lingering musk".

A VOICE IN THE NIGHT

All night long, it lasted,
That terrible retching and moaning.
Far into the night
It lasted,
Even when I plugged my ears
It broke through like a livid scar

A harrowing from Hell,
A curtain of nature torn to shreds,
As the afflicted bullock dropped to its knees,
Unable now to clear its bowel,
Gas rising inside it like a foetid storm.

Neighbours from the valley
Stood and watched, helpless
As the creature twisted, belched and turned
This way, then that, in agony.

We summoned police.
They said they could do nothing.
We called the vet, but he could do nothing.

He explained: "There is no hope.
The creature has swallowed plastic.
A lot of it,

And so it will remain there,
Unless we operate.
Which we cannot do,
For even if we tied it up,
It would break through,
That stuff
Sticks to the gut like glue".

A silence descended.
We stood, shoulder to shoulder,
As witnesses to its terrible end,
Farmers all our lives,
Wondering what to do with this brave
New technology that gave us plastic.

The creature continued
Its cacophony of wailing
Until dawn broke like a smear of glue
over the valley.

And finally, it lay motionless,
And we returned to our Cottage,
Empty bellied, to mourn.

MR PARKINSON IS COMING TO TEA

IN ANCIENT WOODS

Woods near Aylsham, Norfolk, photo by Kelvin I. Jones

In ancient woods we walked often,
You and I,
In summer,
When the Earth was clad in living green,
And birds above us sang
Of how the land once had been
Like a jewel, shining,
Beneath a vast and limitless sky.

We did not pause for long.
We kept an even pace,
For in woods, one can soon be lost,

And the wall
Between the living and the dead
Sometimes thins and disappears;
And then the wood,
Wherein we walk,
Is no longer such a friendly place.

We do not own the woods.
We did not once comprehend.
We misunderstood.

The woods belong to no one.
They, like the ocean,
Are boundless,
Ever renewing;

Full of ghosts of the departed,
Oak, ash, sycamore and yew;
Trees with limbs and eyes,
And sap for blood,
And faces of ruddy hue.

They have been here since the dawn of time,
Standing resolute in shadow,
Groaning as the west winds blow,
Or in winter,
Caked in rime;
But on, eternally on they persist,
Through rain, storm and mist,

MR PARKINSON IS COMING TO TEA

These guardians of the Earth,
Resistant to axe or mortal blow.

As we walk on in silence
Through these dew-soaked woods,
We hear them, whispering
At break of day,
Their voices deep and grey,
Somnolent and slow.

I MUST GO DOWN TO THE GARDEN

Goddess Circe, statue found in garden of my wife's care home, in Liskeard. Photo by Kelvin. I. Jones

I must go down to the garden,
Where the gods and the goddesses lie.
For enchantment there is, in the garden,
Under that dazzling sky.

I shall go down to the garden,
For they say that my memories are there;
And they say that the old ones

MR PARKINSON IS COMING TO TEA

Shall come alive,
Those who are buried deep there.
I must go down to the garden,
For it banishes grief and despair.
I must go down to the garden,
For my heart, it is withering here.

I must go down to the garden,
For the streets are a clattering din,
And when I come to the garden,
The goddess invites me in.

I must go down to the garden,
For the goddess is standing there.
And there are butterflies, nestling in her cheeks,
And birds in her flowing, golden hair.

THE HOODED MAN

The Hooded Man - A Poem, based on a pastel painting, entitled, 'The Hooded Man', also, an original poem by Debbie Jones.

The west wind whispers, the east wind calls,
But the Lord of the Forest shall protect all our souls.

These tall, moss - green trees,
The sentinels of time and space
Have grown here for centuries,
Encircled, scored, made dark by withering leaves,
Turned ochre - brown in winter's grip,
And cruel, but steady march.

MR PARKINSON IS COMING TO TEA

As the world unfrowns from its helmeted
Slumbers,
Shadowy figures rise up before us;
Fingers beckon us from ancient hands.

These trees feel the breath
On their woody limbs;
And in the air about them,
We hear dawn break
In shattered fragments.

The circle now is unbroken;
It turns and spins upon the land.
We hear the winter's weathering pace,
Drumming the earth,
Destroying, but giving rebirth,
A mystic land
To all living creatures who dwell herein.

Lord of the Forest,
Your voice wrapped by burgeoning leaves,
We glimpse your face turned and tanned,
By time and decay,
As the world slowly awakens
Transformed by air, fire, earth and water.

The blind god Odin enters the circle,
His fingers spinning runes from either hand.
We hear him speak and beyond the clouds,

His voice rings loud and razor - clear,

And so we sing and paint, and write,
And journey into this dream-locked,
Moon-lit night,

Or we swim with mermaids,
Far out of sight,
Plundering the whale-riven
shore,

Or lie and dream in leafy eaves,
Of ancient kingdoms,
Their shorelines washed by savage,
Shipwrecking seas.

So we two stand by Herne's old tree,
In this place in the wood,
Set like a jewel in the hills;
Bound by the salty, scrivened sea,
A place of magic,
Where nothing is
what it may seem to be;

Where The Hooded Man
Is slowly but surely,
Carving
The runes of our destiny
Upon his creased and leathery hands,

MR PARKINSON IS COMING TO TEA

Standing as a tree,
In this place of
Quiet, still augury,
This timeless sanctuary.

Oh, Hooded Man,
Of the darkling dell,
Of the shifting mist,
And of mysterious dark caverns,
Set deep into the earth,
Where some say fairy folk
Also do dwell.

So mote it ever be.

DREAMING OF MERMAIDS

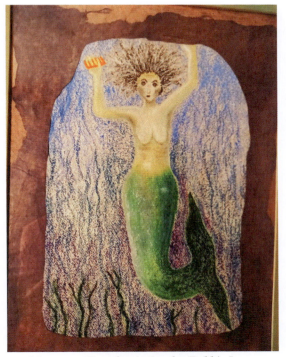

Mercrone. Pastel painting by Debbie Jones.

Last night I dreamed of mermaids,
And when I awoke,
The taste of salt was in my mouth,
And my eyes stung
From the wash of thundering
And mountainous waves.

MR PARKINSON IS COMING TO TEA

Voluptuous and desirable
These creatures were,
With pear-shaped breasts and satin thighs.
They lured me to their dark
And jewel-encrusted kingdom,
From which no man may return.

They led me to a chamber,
A cave that stank of seaweed,
And there, I spoke
To the souls of the departed:

Old, blind Tiresias, the prophet,
Who had lost his way here, long ago,
And the knight, Sir Galahad,
Who had found here at last,
The Holy Grail,

But could never return it,
For the mermaids had crucified him
And put him on a cross
Where he had hung and bled
For centuries.

There were others standing here,
Trapped in that briny
And miasmic gloom;
Priests and politicians,
Poets and false prophets

Of joy and doom;

Murderers and millionaires
Who all had died too soon;
Those who had died, wanting more,
Or those who had swum,
Beyond the shore, in search of heaven,
And found it not;
Finding only a purgatory
Of time forgot.

Here I also found my brother,
In priestly robes, swinging a censer,
Fearful he might not redeem his soul,
Before The Judgement Day,
Before the closing of the gates.

All these had lost their way,
And found they were struck dumb,
When they knelt to pray.

And when I at last awoke,
I found that I lay,
Naked,
Cold and alone
On a bleak and barren shore,
And on my tongue lay a livid scar,
Which was the curse of mermaids.

MR PARKINSON IS COMING TO TEA

In that moment I did know,
Though I might journey far,
Or swim at dead of night,
Far out into the vast, limitless seas,
I would never reach eternity
For I had listened to
Alluring voices, those of
Those of the sirens of the deep;
And thus,
Being lost at sea,
Would ever more weep.

I had seen them
As they drifted,
At the water's edge,
Below and above those deathly waves,
Their wide, scaly tails
Winding voluptuously around me
Moving forth and back.

And the dead men
Who these mermaids had lured
Drowned
Lay like rows of scratched
And pummelled
Scrimshaw
On the scarred and wind-blown sand.

They had heard human voices

Of the living, calling them
To arise and waken,

But heard in their slumber
Only the sirens' call
Of Circe's sisters,
And like me, had given up
Their souls,

And crashed
Amid the thunder
Of approaching storms,
On these black, granite rocks
And drowned.

AHAB IN THE PARK

Line drawing by Douglas Walters.

Yesterday,
When my mind was beset by fear
And the sky lay like grey spittle
On freshly laundered sheets,
I met this old guy in the park.

He was called Anthony.
And he was picking litter

Near to dark.
I asked him why he was doing it
And then he said.

"You're a long time dead.
And I know I won't be coming back.

"Not this side of eternity.
I'm waiting for the minister.
I'm waiting for the chop;
I'm waiting to see if God is like
he's claimed to be.
Like the Sword of Holy Destiny,
The razor blade or the mincer,
Or the knot of the hangman's
Deadly rope and drop.

"You asked me why I tarry here;
I'm going to the place of no return.
Which most do dread and fear.

"I'm going to the stinker.
That place of desolation.
Where the death ship
drops its anchor.
"Don't ask me any questions;
You have no need to ask.
Don't ask me
What I'm doing here.

MR PARKINSON IS COMING TO TEA

Just be on your way and pass.

"I'm from the clinker.
And I'm from the slum.
I am the rejected;
The blind man, deaf and dumb.
So don't ask me where I'm going to.
Be on your way and let me pass".

2.

"I met this old guy on a train.
It never stopped at stations,
And no one would get off.

"A horde of travellers sitting there
Never breathed, but only coughed.
But one man chose to speak with me
In that shuttered, silent train,
That wound its solitary way
Through lands of desolation.

"He said his name was Anthony.
I said it had a nice refrain;
I asked what was his destination;
And the answer came the same.
Please don't ask me any question.
About the name of my terrain.
I'm going to the place whence none return, And

no soul shall remain the same.

"I'm going to the minister.
To have my rights read out;
To a place of uncertainty.
To a land where nothing lasts.
These questions you keep asking.
They are driving me insane.
They have a dark, disturbing quality,
Like an unkindness of Ravens,
Sleek, with black and jagged wings;
And a sinister refrain.

"Listen, and mark me well;
I'm neither in heaven nor in hell.
I'm for the Deathly Hallows
And I'm heading into the dark;
"I'm on the road to Hades.
I won't be coming back,
And I'm standing here on the quayside,
From where the dead embark.

"You asked me my opinion
Of where you think we will go;
It isn't in heaven and it's not to hell.
But this I truly know.
It's the tortured voyage of the seven seas,
Contained in an echoing shell
Where anguished souls drift in foam,

MR PARKINSON IS COMING TO TEA

Lost in eternity.

"It's the wonder of the heavens.
The banshee of the aggrieved.
It's God's deadly weapon,
Where the hangman spins his rope
From faces of the dead,

"And where there is no longer hope,
But only fear and dread.
It's the place where we must suffer
The anger of prophet Job,

"Who challenged God to meet him
In this bleak and lonely place,
Where the Lord God Jahweh
Stood in a bloody robe,
"Cursing the human race;
That place of fear and wonder
Which haunts our waking dreams;
That place which stands in eternity
Neither in time nor space;
Where naught shall ever be the same,
And nothing is what it seems.

"So please don't ask me when or where
Or preach to the unconverted,
Or share with those converted
Your apocryphal tales of resurrection,

For it's more than I can bear".

I stared at his weathered face;
Those sorrowful eyes, the distant stare,
That lined and furrowed brow,
That constant walk
Of dogged and unvarying pace.

Then came a rumble of Thunder,
And thereafter a storm that
Crashed and roared,
And above the noise and turmoil,
I saw the sea whiplash,
Striking passing ships.
Driving them onto the barren rocks,
Where they lay, torn and smashed.

And I saw God's red and bloody son,
Emerging from that maelstrom.
And I saw on his hands the marks of nails,
And on his face was the dust of the tomb.
And then I saw what all men saw,
On that barren road to Golgotha
At the festival of Eostre,
Where folk once gathered to celebrate
Before the Romans vanquished the druids
And peace was replaced by slavery and hate;
As from a distant shore, we all did see

MR PARKINSON IS COMING TO TEA

Rising up from the rolling waves,
The shadow of Captain Ahab.
His bloody body cold,
Lying on upon his ravaged back,
Harpooned, held fast, trapped,
By tormented dreams
Of the blistered,
wounded white whale
And of how he might have redeemed himself,
But now lay doomed to eternity.

That great leviathan had lured him
to this dark and rocky place
Where sailors' bodies float and drown
And restless spirits walk apace.

Ahab was crying out to God,
But none heard him
Mid the waves piled high with dead sea birds
And mermaids' glistening but deadly tails,
Above the jetsam
And the strewn sea wrack,
And leg bones of long, dead men
Twisting and hurling the lashing waves
From salty white to black.
God listened not to Ahab.
For he had run out of luck.
He wasn't listening to anyone,
For He gave no favour

To the plans of Ahab
Or those cursed by fate.

God stood, listening to no one
On deck with the Hallows crew,
Staring into the face of hell,
Watching the monstrous Leviathan
As its body plunged beneath the waves,
Then rose afresh from the saline foam,
Its eyes a piercing blue
In that place of fallen Eden,
That other, dreadful place.

That wizened, ravaged wasteland,
Where litter wraps its hands
Round stained and pockmarked lamp posts,
Where no birds sing
And harvests dwindle to husks;

That wizened, ravaged wasteland
Where skies are a sullen gray;
And shaped like cancerous tumours,
By the dead on Judgment Day;

Where the souls of the newly risen
Stand and tremble on this desolate track

In mortal dread of the carrion crows
That gather, chattering at their backs.

MR PARKINSON IS COMING TO TEA

These weary travellers,
Picking up litter here and there
In the gathering dark.
Standing close together,
Watching the fading, setting sun
As light thins to strips of pallid blue,

Those long lost men and women;
The redeemers; the poets, the painters,
And the dreamers.

Those who have lost their bearings,
Looking for answers to questions
But finding none.

For we, the crew of The Pequod,
Who bore witness to the Nazarene
As he cried out to His Father in despair,
As he hung there upon the Rood,

None of us did God spare,
Save I, Ishmael, who saw it in a vision,
As I sat on the deck to pray
To the ancient gods
Of wind and storm;

I alone bore witness and was spared.

SELDEN

Selden,
The Notting Hill murderer,
Was seldom to be seen
Here on the dark, fog-bound Moor,
Though one man had seen him,
Walking as if in a dream
Of the dreadful crimes
That still assailed and haunted him.

Here, where the seven black crows
Gathered in a line,
Their ragged voices
Mocking him,
Spitting at him
Cursed names
From long ago.

Like that of the damned rapist,
The cruel and wicked Hugo
Who, on one cold Michaelmas night,
When the moon shone upon the moor
In an unearthly silver light,

And good folk were told not to stray
From the moorland path

MR PARKINSON IS COMING TO TEA

That by Hound Tor did lay,
For fear the Devil might steal their souls
And they would suffer for eternity,
Behind these stark and riven granite walls.

Aye, they had seen him,
Selden,
Staring out from the rocks,
Crying, sometimes moaning,
His mournful eyes hollow, lost,
Like a thing possessed.

For the madman Selden
There never could be rest
For his loved ones
He'd left dying,
For those he'd maimed and brained,
For those he'd stabbed and cleft.

On the night Selden died
There was only one sound.
It was not
The booming of a bittern
Nor the shrieking of a pony
As it foundered, then drowned
Beneath the morass of the great
Grimpen Mire,
Where, it is said,
The dead do lie forever

With their tongues as black as liver
And their lungs half expired.

No, this was a dread, unearthly sound,
As if the dead had all risen
From the churchyards on the Moor
And joined with that devil dog
They had seen so oft before,

At the eery breaking of the dawn
When all lay soft and moist
And uncannily grey.

They say that Death had come for him
To rip from him his heart,
To serve his master pale and grim,
Carrying his sharpened scythe
Along these Grimspound paths.

And others do say,
Here in Princeton prison,
That, though on that day of reckoning
Each soul will duly have arisen,
There is one that shall be missing,
And that he shall have no blessing,

For Selden often walks here
On such a night like this,
When the harrowing wind doth cruelly bite

MR PARKINSON IS COMING TO TEA

And the rank bog doth smell of piss.

You may see his white face
Set hard there as fractured bone,
Or glimpse his sad reflection
On a shattered sarsen stone;

For you know
What good folk do say on the Moor
And you know that it be true,
That the Devil Dog shall rule his own,
And on rank, mist - drenched nights like this,
When the east wind doth shriek and moan,
Selden shall march forever in their midst,
With that dead, demented crew.

They say that Death had come for him
To rip from him his heart,
To serve his master pale and grim;
Carrying his sharpened scythe
Along these Grimspound paths;

And others do say
Here in Princeton prison,
That though on that day of reckoning
Each soul will have arisen,
There is one that shall be missing,
And that he shall have no blessing,

For Selden often walks here
On such a night like this
When the cruel wind doth cruelly bite
And the rank bog doth smell of piss,

You may see his white face
Set hard there as stone,
Or glimpse his sad reflection
On a shattered sarsen stone,
For you know
What they say on the Moor
And you know that it be true,
That the Devil Dog shall rule his own,
And on rank, mist drenched nights like this
Selden shall march forever
In their midst,
With that dead, demented crew.

MR PARKINSON IS COMING TO TEA

'Selden Possessed,' pen and watercolour by Douglas Walters.

Printed in Great Britain
by Amazon